Scented Rushes

Scented Rushes

Nada Gordon

ROOF BOOKS
NEW YORK

ISBN 13: 978-1-931824-40-8
Library of Congress Catalog Card Number: 2010934723

Cover photograph, "The Sorrows of Not-So-Very-Young Nada" by Gary Sullivan;
design & collages by Nada Gordon

Versions of these poems first appeared in *Mrs. Maybe, Sprung Formal, Aufgabe,* and *Peep/
Show: a Taxonomic Exercise in Textual and Visual Seriality.* Thanks to the kind editors.

Thanks to Marianne Shaneen, Stan Apps, Dana Ward, Rodney Koeneke, Brandon
Downing, Drew Gardner, Abigail Child, Adeena Karasick, Toni Simon, Stephanie
Young, Mónica de la Torre, Marilyn Gordon, and ... Gary Sullivan.

Roof Books are distributed by
Small Press Distribution
1341 Seventh Avenue
Berkeley, CA 94710-1403

Phone orders: 800-869-7553
www.spdbooks.org.

This book was made possible, in part, with public funds from
the New York State Council on the Arts, a state agency.

State of the Arts

NYSCA

ROOF BOOKS
are published by
Segue Foundation
303 East 8th Street
New York, NY 10009
www.seguefoundation.com

➣ Scented Rushes

"Oh, please! There are some
scented rushes!" A sudden transport
of delight. "There really are — and such

beauties!" "No, but I meant — please,
may we wait and pick some?"
The boat was left to drift down,

till it glided gently in among the waving
rushes. The little arms were plunged in
elbow-deep, to get hold of the rushes

a good long way down before breaking
them off. Just the ends of her tangled hair
dipping into the water — while with bright

eager eyes she caught at one bunch after another
of the darling scented rushes. "Oh, what a lovely
one! Only I couldn't quite reach it."

And it certainly did seem a little provoking
("almost as if it happened on purpose," she thought):
there was always a more lovely one that she couldn't

reach. "The prettiest are always further!" she said
at last with a sigh at the obstinacy of the rushes
in growing so far off. Flushed cheeks and dripping

hair and hands. And these, being dream-rushes,
melted away almost like snow,
as they lay in heaps at her feet ....

from Chapter 5, "Wool and Water," *Through the Looking Glass for my imaginary friend*

⋟ *Never Contents*

I. CUCKOO

II. ERMINE

III. AGALMA

⪼ O Curator! O My Curator!

O Curator! O my Curator!
Take these nude growls
spun in addiction
as you will, as breath vacuumed
out of me and louchely reshaped.
The star heart bears each other out
and put you there (surly) instead.
Duckling imprintation. An excess
of imagination. It's true I have
a small but raucous head,
thick with saucy reverie.
O man of Remember, dear
mandarin, how you slanted
through the air! (Do you care?)
Yellow leaf dance autumnal winds
tell me the innermost feeling:
those "wrinkled wildfires" unreel
as cuckoo joy rides in this shaky
musical formality—or what's
a maelstrom for? Roar. Plink.
All the flowers now are singing:
        "truth"
        "dream"
        "think the boyfriend"
in the smooth Crisco of this
ancient flame language.

Well, these are the limits of the earth singer
and her (my) words are vapid pluots held
against the arrows of the Venus Exchange
and the gleaming monstrosity of you.
Stupid Cupid. Negative youth in don't
(*don't*: the Casio is *too loud*), storming
a small small nuptial chamber
as fey and clownish toy dogs, but
I, with imaginary coffee
on the stained wall of lovely feeling,

only I'm making any noise. Listen!
O, O, send me the gentleman!
Please send me the gentleman!
So too you harden (harden).
The month circle flower is good,
for we are all biological, moist
with pores, taut with musculature,
buzzed with electricity, etc.: *you, too*.

Darkling, we're both oldly singular
as cicadas slurring the trees. Doesn't
the rocket launcher want to
cuddle up to the shiny rocket?
You could even say it glows.
The torture, the torture is red —
a red flower (of course) —
so I bear down on mortality's hard edge
with my quizzical "sex face."

O my absent pictograph, dear
mean cipher, a few setting suns is red.
Do not abandon me: OK, so bye.
We're in language as tapeworms,
but language is in me as balady.
The tonight is rain again, and
(I said this before) whatever I lost
I just … lost. There's a light drizzle
out suburb way; you're a scratchy overlay …
I beg you to cheat, I cheat after all
remembering fondly, corallinely
all these lustrous clothes.
If I project too deeply it's as a
jeweled nightingale, so I search
the nightmare dream park
for the bleating clarity of thought
and steal from the person of the heart
his lambent, cranky possibility.

Do not go home today!
The sun flies through the air
as if to jump on you.

"Be crazy about." I resemble fog
in order to resemble spending again
that day near the juniper trees,
astounded by clouds.
The moon resembles the lemon
or war-torn palimpsest of this
vagrant singing (signing) girl (me).
O red water lily and floating ridicule,
return to me to the love
of druggy images.
I pour honey down a well.
What else can I do?
O Curator! My Curator!
"I _____ you:
go to _____!"

cuckoo

a parasitic songster

➤ *I'm Truly Searing, Dear*

I lay my view upon a witty formalist, where only wolves and deserted
 playthings live.
I ask my solar plexus, " is this a triangle within liquescence?"
Whenever the mangle shines behind clowns,
And the easterly word dancing over the roans.
I'm truly scarlet, dear,
My life only a piece of pageantry, that needs words, to describe a
 laciness.
In this turbid gaiety, I shall wait for your light intercourse,
A light which gives me your hunger:
Above other lures,
You make a wrestle of life.

⟫ Don't Cry for Me, Mediocrity

I was wondering if you could annoy me in this life . . .

Dampening, this secretion when liars and phonies won't simper,
Although the mooning had become a subset to me,
It would be better if I don't meet a rationale forever.
Don't cry for me, mediocrity:
My love is only for my dairy,
A dairy that's written within tears of lyricism,
One latitude for you and one for me,
Even just the one norm without the sounds of warning.
Darling, your stigmata unite within the light of hornrims:
Only pure hair futilely wins and lives.

➣ *Would You Promise to Whelm Me Under the Screw?*

Will there be sounds that belong to our fortress?
Have you ever fall into loops with me?
The flowers desperate to give their best pretense.
In one narrative under the laboratory of life,
Will there be tortoises that give us love?
The sea waves rolling to the shocks,
And the scarification had made us shy.
If … and if I am someone else,
Would you promise to love me under the leathery eggs?

➤ *Darling, I Made You Up*

The scars that swoon beneath the beauty of marriage,
One and only cackling that left in your every grimace,
Dreaming and a dream of your room,
A song from the fairy of the falsest time,
Whenever our headsets joined in unity of vanity,
Wherever the cranky and flirtatious dancing.
Darling, you know that I miss you in this cramp of love,
Although the wound trying to sing,
And the soreness become my paramour,
I shall not feed until my last breast falls away.
We'll be droning all night together,
On one lovely purple feather ....

➳ *Wherever You've Found Our Stain Behind the Moon*

The night fish has its creepy smile beyond the under-light of
   pluperfect sundown.
Whenever easterly breeze mothers calling your threatening name,
Wanna touch your basic hand within the pudding of love,
Even though I can't see like a wilting mumble our stain
   behind the moon,
My least dearest tele-valentine.
My tele-life and tele-destiny,
One violet tear can't hold this burden of vinegary love.
There you're walking with the marmot cry of the marmot sky.
Let me join the wilting mumble within,
wherever you've found our stain behind the moon ....

⇒ *Bifurcate Me, My Diversion*

We leap on someone, but when the time passing by, we don't know why, and she/
he still doubt on us. Why?

Don't you see one lens in your hibernation?
While the pangolin gives its bleating to us
In the lenis of an adventurousness
There was when our logics met

Dearest contagion
See how high explosive my love for you
Like a rebuttal flows into the argument
and the lotus sing a lotus song for you

Come with me, my calamitous one
Say it in the power of letdown
Where the moon is no more powdery than your sternness
A feeling that unties our discharge

Believe me, my disciplinarian
Like the argument of the sunset
It is you in my head.
Really, it's not a plume of feathers, especially on a helmet,
    or a dashing elegance of manner,
      or a brownish-gray or golden horse "of a dovelike color"
      that has a silvery-white or ivory mane or tail.

⤳ *Whenever I Waver Between Two Rathers*

Whenever I wither between two reality shows
I see beautiful green goddesses along the way.
Its lighten up by the tulips.
I ask myself, "Is this my crybaby?"
Whenever the wincing left me behind.
All just a open blur to a storm that zithered
Mein kopf, wishing you are helium with me.
Hear! The crickets are dreaming to say love.
Please, don't libel me,
Hold my ideas and you'll see the petulance of life with me.

⇒ *My Dexadrine, I Am So Wistful Like Amber in the Rumpus*

O starling, say it scratchy to me,
Scratch your lowing hands out beneath the bless of love:
Were there lies on desertion?
Through the screen, I look upon the lies.
My überman, you are so b-rated just like a raging under,
Where all the buds are bound to be humiliated.
One doubt underneath your bootsteps that flustered and fly away,
As your tears had bring the diary into lissome pretension.
I … I will be your thoughts in goats,
Wherever pains are gone and there are smiling motors.

➣ *Wherever Virility Spreads its Muses*
or
➣ *You Are Ambiguous Just Like Leeches in the Dusk*

Today my head is documentary, the crowd from the house party still makes me want to dance until my body divulged.

Bird of ill omen, one more time,
Whenever the sow still dance,
Wherever virility spreads its muses,
You are the ones among angelfishes.
Can a splash of water ruining a painting of liver?
Baby, you are anhedonic just like lilies in the doctrine.
How I beg the mood to come,
And toughen my deepest hankering.
Kiss my lap, birdie, and feel the existentialism of love,
I was and always belong to you, my lyre.

➤ *My Dogstar, Don't Laugh at Me*

My derangement, lumpen beneath our dumbest memories,
One torch beneath the sun in angst,
Our lip inside the brightest soma.
Shy through the beauty of the mawkishness,
I was lie down in the greedy grassland;
Stretch my hair out to seek a paradox,
Your sham —your friable patter— hold me tight in this lava.
My darkling, don't leave me,
I am only like the worm without a burning conclusion,
A king without its cable,
In the phooey condescension of wryness.

➤ *Is Nourish a Noisy Quarrel?*

Is nourish a noisy quarrel?

Mature size of a foxes?

What are some dialogues that show irony?

Why grooming is important in aviation?

What is the voice of the girl the lovely?

What did Mary Wollstoncraft argue for?

How do you use being?

What is the definition of a boyfriend?

Who wrote an elegy?

What is the phobia of being nervous?

Where do clown tiger came from?

What is smooth interpersonal relations?

Pictures of different relations between living things?

How love become?

⇒ *Big Head, Please Don't Be Urbane Because of Me*

I know exactly what I did to you, since the beginning of torquing time, everything seems just get into wrong delectation. And now, all I am asking to you is I want to see the front matter, not those psychic energizers anymore.

Whenever reindeers calling me out,
"Can you fear me?" all just an attack to my heart,
Even though it seems only theatre can.
For I can't reach the beautiful dramatic monologues with you again.
Baby, please don't be unctuous because of me,
Like white seals expecting sea wine touch its outer line,
The shimmying sky during repugnancy,
And I wish the wind would bring you to the licking,
Where our joy reflects in a smirk,
A melody over vices of meadowlarks.

➣ I Need Your Prurient Lantern

When the noxiousness lie down beside me,
When the meek and staring are shimmying brightly,
You'll make my lines become so lovely,
A gargoyle of love poems that I adore.

Don't you know that I am a 'pataphysicist?
Really, I need your prurient lantern,
To pacify me from your mishearings,
And glide me to be your santa of love,

Show me the weirdness,
Prove me for your energetic lilt.
By the time I try,
To call your narrative with one and only loudness through me.

➤ Love Me With the Photics of Marginalia

I walk through the template of lads, where your name still frightens my mind,
and the sulky marmots tell a story about falsetto . . .

Give me vibraphones which it's a warm of your love,
Give me sand dollars so I can hold to cover my feeling,
Miss me if I am gone, "one whose appearance causes a grimace."
Love me with the pessary of moping,
For a digression without digression,
Just like lumps that shed from its therapy,
Can we see a sarcasm once more?
Wherever ducks and nightwalkers sing?
O … Mumbled brute, give me a love,
Until my eyes can't speak hymen anymore.

❧ *Why Don't You Love Me Blankness?*

If I can sing a song about ligatures,

There will be bitterness and butteriness among the flounces,

Harangues and power of love-in-a-mist together in me,

Though it's only safety pins that accompany me in drawls.

Discord, why don't you love me blankness?

Did the bemazement of love had deceived you?

All these microcosms of songbirds make me sick,

If and only if, I can transpose your heat in you,

I will look upon the scrawls and say, "Gush, for Thy had bind us in
  plethora."

Don't have anything but two heavens open to war:

How long must I wait to sing in the radiator and relume?

Only sheen gives ardor to a croon in this twinkly holomorph.

➣ I am fulfilled with the smell of jungle, try to find why the song still sways behind the clumps, and why troglodytes seem have no desire to live, here I am in nowhere jungle, recasting all melodies

Damply, whenever singing bitches calling your bluff,
The beauty of your self-regard has refried a love of mine
In the scuffs of light, sweet, crude lips.
A seabird moment can change a destiny of love.
Hear baby, the wind flew the loves up and go away
Just like the libertines try to survive in this winter.
I am senseless baby, I can only see the bad nodes
Even though I am a man and a dreamer.
Still my view lies in the least reason
Just where the snail falls from the eye of the sun.
(I light into you, and I always do)

◆ Don't Listen to Me

Darling, I am hebephrenic. Please … Please for the sake of levitation, come
blearily to me

Whenever the mundanity leans in my head,
I'll weep here until my tag clouds run dry.
If the skink won't live in the winsome forest anymore,
I'll jump in a weird arrangement with you, my curator.
Wherever the swallow from the deepest handwringing that ever exist,
Could it be one single lisp that thrown away from our organs?
I … I wish I can answer that,
Although my hands can reach the white sound and hold it tinkling.
It seems only your semantics that left,
Baby please don't lurch from me ….

⋙ *How Do I Tickle?*

I don't know, vertigo
Every sooty charmer
Asking questions
Why and why?

I walk to the blameless city
Try to find out the possums
Love's bent knee in my pants
Don't know, vertigo

I fall in love across him
A beautiful girl in my tights
Filling a lactation in my heart
Until my last boyhood
Fever

This brutishness
As sweaty as my mane
Where do I cerebrate?
So hard to say …
laterally …

◕ *I Need Your Leitmotif*

When I create you
I can't fake my hard-on:
Never find someone that fanatic
It's really a lorikeet

Knock on your head once more
Maybe one day
If I become an ape of love
I could make you slap-happy

This love
Bothering inside me
Full of ire
Spazzing all of my time

Dazzling
You know that I need your larynx
Can't gaze at you so long
And look at this poem so meteorically

O ... Love me like an intriguing notion
Love me *velvet-creepily*
Search my sour turmoil ...

I try to write you down my frantic annotations
into the bottom of honey till there's no more travesty

⤜ *Lovely Human*

I am not an Exoskeleton.

Prancing as if I am a prancer
Sallow with great desire
I am not an exoskeleton
Replicate me as I am should be

Love makes me wander
Walking around the corn
Finding hidden holes

Is love only for Mexicans?

ᴂ *A Thin Line Which Is Flat*

On this rancor, I am stunning to see a beautiful irruption,
Surrounded by murk which glows in this hulk.
Fascinated by flaws of drooping wimples,
A loser writes the feelings into a thin line which is flat.
Lives of bread make harmony in morons.
Throughout the blood veil, it gives love.
I wish I can hear the locust flowers sing,
And they will not stop me to drip on everything.

➤ You Are Labyrinthine, My Friend

This evening I am dwarfing, whether I choose or not, an ontology is not a thing that we must rely on, but you, you are labyrinthine, my friend!!

Clop, clop, narcotic, narcotic,
From the ovary until the bright stars,
its shantung still remains in my satyr's hips
I was chosen by the cynical lilt
To the ravine of antic math—we both seek for it —
You are lateral, my friend.
Strangle my weirdness, as if the love is under
the basically humorous watertowers.
It is because one good drunk wants to pass
as a male or be transformed into one
Through unguent, farm machinery hands.
My friend, don't leak appetite in your persistent hipness:
Hold it, and it will be anguished and biologically yearny
Just as the whimper of morning,
like a traditional indication of gender,
        sucks.

⮞ *Please Perplex Me*

My sweet destruction, whenever tears become the indulgence of
    horseplay,
I shall laugh within four billion and forty years,
Just when the dawn expects me nothing but montage.
Through the shine of an extremely complicated montaged sun,
I shall rejoice within zealous breeze,
My spotted dog, you are collapsed to me,
Let me creep along the horizon of the damp, grey, meshes,
Let me steal the old masters as far as the fictional sun.
Please come back to me, my editor.
I will listen to a black harmony of conglomerates,
Crucified underneath the rebellion of your sound effects,
And among the self-referential bruise seekers,
I am not 76 minutes of unvarying solid blue light.

➤ *Ovaltine Love Feeling*

The beauty of love that I feel in mimic of eyes' slippage
Into the "cubistic environment" of my soul
As if my body ripped the experienced chaos of everyday life
By the deepest of love's neglected child.

Understanding love as a more fundamental set of dualisms
Translate life into a visual corollary of a word trap:
A perfect feeling like an echo chamber.
There's nothing impossible: I work with ephemera.

⋑ *Let the Boys Sing About Me*

In the Name of Antinomy

Here I am wilting
Here I forget who I am
In the name of antinomy
There's no more sideways blanking out

Falling blown into crust
Crawling towards obscenity
Ruffle-me-not
Uncomplicated lamb

In the name of karaoke
Let me lip-sync once more
The frothing sigh
Only one is my wife

Let the boys sing about me
One bad history
And if minds turn slack
into its purée
Will you be my cast-iron brassiere?

➤ Release My Wilder Pop

Suddenly he come back into your eye after he broke your handkerchief a long time ago …

My feedback loop
I write this reeking
With arias

Why so many balls
This reeking
Sound of you
Pulp that full of redness

My loop
Fulfill my blushing denial
To you alone

Why so hard to even squeak
this loop
Let me sour
And release my wilder pop.

(what are you gonna do?)

➣ *Sing with Your Rarebit Vices*
or
➣ *Look at Me*

Love
Sing with your rarebit vices
Greedy
To yell you

Missing you
flying free in spuds
fallen furbelows
Semiosis of nastiness come over me

Say it my love
Your smile full of evacuation information
Must love be bickered over
In teardrop worms?

Only one weirdness:
I want you to shrink it.
Look at me.

➤ *Please Usufruct to Me*

This evening, I am so livid just like beavers in the mystery . . .
Suddenly my eyes seem so much jawbone to come. . . But, without humming . .

Baby, every time I look into the wax lip mouth,
Is your image that reflects in my heebie-jeebies.
Should I say "gross" to the tricks in the inspiring machine?
Words of love are just as the seared in the hardness of lover.
Flying up hard to heathens,
Lay my vehemence to the yeasty horizon.
Baby, please come blistering to me.
I come in my mouth, breathe in tears of lassi.
Please, leer at my hump,
I shall waiting for you at the end of the wrong number.

ermine

Let the fauves be my witnesses.

☙ The Fine Romance of the Three Smiles

A pomegranate that no one admired
I can only sigh and pity myself

Nightingale's speech in the scented garden
Sitting down and scrutinizing him

Seeing he is so refined
It seems such a perfect match

Three smiles at Hiqiu locked me in love
Three locks of love shackling my soul.

Mistake me not for a wanton man,
my love for you are sincere

I ponder as I grind the ink,
How many would pursue me like that?

His poetry and painting are splendid
A scholar like him is good

The young masters ordered me to get ginseng
We'll seal our love in the Peony Pavilion

Autumn Fragrance, don't go!
He dares to entice my pageboy.

Slowly pacing her lotus steps
Heart beating wildly

In shyness and glad beauty,
She takes the seal with joy and fear

The fine romance of the three smiles
Will be forgotten for all posterity

⮷ Condiments

I can't ketchup to you
to sweetly relish
your interiorities:
not even with this light
pelvic mayonnaise. The poems
are the crucial chutney
to the bland daily "special."
Nothing else matters,
not the wasabi
of your personality,
the coarse mustard
of my mannered
suggestiveness,
or the gooey duck sauce
of these noxious phantasms.

grrr

These callipygian longings.
Not to have seen you naked =
the greatest injustice known
to man! But don't assume
that I am writing about
you.

Stunned daffy energy
morphosing on the lipid
pleasure of revolution
in tartan tights. I love
it when men tell me what
to do I love the timid crust
of need on the surface
of false order. There.
You have your orders.
Go.

Life beribboning
itself with more
and more and more life:
then twisting into its
same old spiral.
In semicostume as always
prying the sticky lens
from the bioglobe.
Opinionated. Injured.
All the little …
comptrollers …

⋙ *Here in the Gynaeceum*

Today I feel like … a large group of worms
with a flattened, unsegmented body, fleshy
and flawed and desirous of exaggerated
compliment. Fluttering or waving freely,
gaudy, ostentatious, conspicuous, and
impudent, my wingless wings are firm
and pulpy, like fruit, or like fleams,
especially those used for opening veins.
I am rigid and pliant, stiff and easily
bent, capable of modification by a group
of yellow pigments or a person who
flattens something. I guess that means
I am a Flathead, erroneously named by
confusion and marked by my windiness
of speech. I vulcanize a whole new rubber
tread on the bare underlayer of the fabric
of this verse, like a signal given by a drum or
bugle or a bend or turn as in a line or
wall. What is done in revenging puts a new
vamp on savagery, but with a dull or rounded
apex that draws back the veil of inadvertence
and undergoes diminutive revving. It vamps
again or anew, falling into an earlier, worse,
or less complex condition, like the flesh
at the edge of an incision that can be retracted,
or drawn back in, as in claws. High-pitched,
shrill, piercing, brilliant, intense, as a sharp flash
of light, it passes close to or skims the surface in
opposite directions parallel to the plane of the contact,
causing it to flow in a stream or fall in drops, let flow or drop,

send forth or spread about, or cause to flow off without
penetrating. Today I am about the size of a pigeon
and am related to the petrels and albatrosses, like
a leaf base enveloping a stem of grass, or membrane
around a muscle. She is the nominative case form,
her the objective, her or hers the possessive, and herself
the intensive and reflexive, except as in, "our dog is a she."
This is a collection of sheeny things bound together, partly shaved,
like a regular fem or female animal: severe, intense, acute;
strong, biting and pungent; a kind of daisylike chrysanthemum
breaking or bursting into pieces suddenly. Here in the gynaeceum
I, costumed as a person or persons whose appearance or habits
are like those of a gypsy, release combinations that are free
to turn in any direction and will keep their original plan of rotation
no matter which way the wheel is turned. A circular or spiral motion;
whirl. Revolution. Vortex. Coil. (see *tugging at the ear in perplexity*)

⮡ *Poem to Myself*

You make me tired with your long, curly
reddish brown hair and ironic ideology;
you are a short syllable that should be long,
your stupid plan is "very clever" and your I.Q.
is white, malleable, and ductile, like inflammation
of the eye or Romanian paralysis. OK, so you're
"heated with radiant energy"; so what?
Could be a seaweed dried and bleached
for use as a medicine, or a very large, heavy, powerful
dog with a hard rough coat, formerly used in hunting
a combination of circumstances or a result
that is the opposite of what might be expected or
what might be considered appropriate. A rainbowlike
show or play of colors is a kind of locomotive made of
fool's gold, implying mental unsoundness and an
utterly illogical nature of that which is directly
contrary to reason, i.e. a round, pigmented membrane formed
of meat, potatoes, carrots, onions, and other vegetables.
You are tiresome, troublesome, tedious, quick-tempered,
silver-edged, Maltese, and conspicuous, like the apparent
enlargement of a brightly lighted object seen against
a dark background. Construed as *sing*, O little stain made
by rust or ink, you've got yr Irish up—for what? O Senecans,
Mohawks, Tuscarorans, Oneidas, Cayugas, Onandagas, Cherokees,
feign ignorance of this sinking fireboat, her tubular integers,
her infantile ballistic organization, grey like freshly broken
cast iron irenic muscles, her degenerate method a creeping
plant with showy leaves and trumpet-shaped prosody
enclosing all of the body but the head. *Ipsissima verba!*

⤳ *Ding*

Amy Winehouse lines her eyes
with the penis of mayhem:
a woman on the subway
plucks her beard. Anus fully
occupied by peace medallion,
like turquoise man-bracelets,
like ding, like sich.

The letter C first makes me
think of abjection — no not
first, or second, but third.
Hunched over in illness or in
laughter: take that, Abulafia!

Transforming the letters into prinking
nightmares. Autistic constant
biting with the lower jaw
and a blunt tonguing the air —
and this is compulsion, too.
This is composition, too.

Anus medley — shouting the sprout,
as the eyes grow tails. I like tuna
salad but not tuna.

The stock market sez: the poetry
is sublime, castles burning, etc.
They can't take this sucky shit —
womanhood — away from me.

⇒ *Exene Dress*

Hot like a kitty / flat like a sound
crowded like a toolkit

vapidity of love as polemic,
I'm an eminent sore, sticking
out. Semiticism of rapid conversation:
sore caves, sore curves, sore flatness. soreness.
Porn girl looks up at camera for a sec, then gets back to business.
The misty mountains are misaligned. Explain.

Barack Obama drinks a Bud Lite.
Everything too meaningful, like panties
on a lamb (wilder). Lernen Sie Englisch, yeah, OK.
Millions old every month
confusing MIDRASH and MIDRIFF.
I cover my cleavage out of respect for others …

Like bobby pins on a yarmulke, these are the days of our "lives":
neurotic golden behavior as sought-for hornbill

EAT the candle: PRAY the html
love whimpering mightily

rocks tumble into hipsters
underwear now in a spoon.

mind asks for a different dogstar
because quiddity is so serviceable

and then I want quince. Jerking.

➤ *Foreign Body Sensation Remix*
(after Charles Bernstein)

Such thrills as chide me fold away
in the indulgent catachresis of male
dismay. Most arduous
of all, distractions:
the band, of minds, makes faces
in sensuous confusion
to face the mates. Entering more
quickly than diction might undo, a glib
of digital croons audience to mother
on. The clacking
of this indignity reduces
for a pittance what lurkers ask
askew. Stochastic
burps, designed in arms, will savor
for its Asians arts and
salaams. Aviaries
know the slice of mom.

Yet hand-cocked bijouteries
refer to what
they want, prestidigitated
slamdunks, queering
humps. Boys
to anger for
a spanking, hieratic
peals incarnadine,
beds betrayed (sashayed)
inside whose harm?

➤ *Unprofessional*

(after Rudyard Kipling)

On what system is this dam' dynamo of our universe wound?

On what he called 'muckings' (like a walrus affronted)?

That's eye-strain! The big voice quavered:

"I've been trying to disentangle the minor interferences
by returning once more to the legitimate drama of cultures."

"Midnight? Oh, certainly, but I'll have to warn my anaesthetist
and reverently return some lenses to their velvet shrines."

A doe with a plum-coloured saddle is squeaking.
She strives desperately to work through the wires
with semitransparent hand-like forefeet.

"In convulsion?"

"She's not! She's all astray,
external to this swab of culture which we call our world.
We're in for a wildish time. She's a woman—not a white mouse!"

Still, he jerked it up, his palm beneath her chin—with male horror.

Then came the explosion of natural human wrath, and
now she goes about like a smiling sheep.

"'It wasn't worth it," was the light answer. "Just hysteria" …
when like a string she relaxed:

the vacuoles—the empty centres—do not take stain,
the vasts of the Ultimate Heavens
fizzing in spirals

singing, "Time Sucks, but Space is Okay."

➤ *Apex of the O*

Well its been a while since I have posted anything personal. Thats because I had to do some things for school that were pretty stressful.

The fact is, though, I Am Obsessed With Natural Hair

And I am obsessed with this piñata. This Piñata is so chilled it never even changes out of these stripy pajamas.

I am also Obsessed with Blinkies! Blinkies is my new passion. I have learned how to make them but I don't have a bunch yet, so I am mixing them in with the others.

I am obsessed with twilight am I weird?

Michael Jackson question: I am obsessed with Michael Jackson. Does anyone know a song I can do for a dance about being obsessed with Michael Jackson?

Why I am obsessed with my doctor? Why I am obsessed with my doctor? Why I am obsessed with my doctor?

I am terribly obsessed with the Carpenters. Ever since I saw Superstar: The Karen Carpenter Story, I've been obsessing on the Carpenters.

Maybe it's because I am obsessed with the grammar of others.

I am obsessed with guns. I think they look so AWESOME I collect as many models as I can. And on TV when a gun is shown for not even half a second, I will immediately know what it is. I only need to see a small portion of it to know! Any one else like me?

Me, I am obsessed with Yorkie Talk.

I love everyone here! I have met so many nice people! I am obsessed with this forum. My friends, in lecture, catch me browsing this website instead of paying attention to the professor … and I smile and say "I love these people!" Thank you for being wonderful. People are so very kind here and we all share love of Yorkies. If I wasn't so tight-up with work, I would spend a lot more time right here with you guys.

I am obsessed with hipsterdom. I don't know why, or what to do about it. I am not a hipster. I never have been.

'I am obsessed with Aishwarya'

Delhi girl Shweta Bhardwaj, who has been tagged as the 'desi Lara Croft' because of her action scenes in Mission Istanbul, says she is obsessed with Aishwarya Rai. "I am obsessed with her and was very sad to know that she got married," said the 21-year-old, adding "If I would have been a boy, I would have definitely married her."

I am obsessed with women's breasts—and it's becoming a problem. When a woman talks to me I can't help myself staring at her chest.

I am not "obsessed with the underworld," though—I am obsessed with my heart.

What am I obsessed with? I am Obsessed with buggys
Check out dunebuggy.com. Just about anything about dune buggies can be found there.

I have to tell you I am obsessed with my childhood. I never pooped. I'm serious, I hated pooing, I never did it. I refused to poo as child.

How to say I am obsessed with you my darling. How do you say I am obsessed with you my darling in different languages translation.

I am obsessed with WALNUTS!! I've got to quit buying them!!!!!! : eek: oh and also I am obsessed with devilled eggs.

I am obsessed with submissive males and couples the kinkier the better

Hi
I am obsessed with chickens, lemons, and not spelling words corecty.

I dont smoke
i have a dog named bingo

i am scared of computer pop-ups
i have parakeets
1 sun condor
favorite food = PASTA

what are you obsessed with? (so grateful to be Mormon!)
I am obsessed with lotion and vaseline. Seriously. I cannot go very
long without lotioning my hands and feet. And the vaseline?

My relationship with the number 23 began several years ago. I was
first introduced to the magick number in the early '90's via Psychick
TV. They where a well know underground band from the U.K. who
did some pretty funky things. The lead singer Genesis P. Orridge
(yes that really was his name) has some really interesting theory on
this number. In short he pointed out to me that 23 is not like all of the
other numbers out there. While my take on 23 is a little different than
his, I am obsessed with the number 23 because I see it frequently in
a variety of random and rather ordinary situations. I see the number
so often that it simply does not make sense, and cannot rationally be
explained. This situation then in turn reminds me that everything
doesn't make sense in the world. That there are some things which
are beyond our understanding. This then leads to a state of not-
knowing where you simply don't try and understanding something
(whether that be a person, a situation or an event) but simply be with
it. This quality of not knowing or unexplaining is a liberating feeling
/ experience. To be able to abandon the habitual need to understand
everything then allows each one of us to authentically experience the
world free of preconceived notions. This is the mind state I want to
be in all of the time, but generally only occasionally touch on. So by
noticing the number 23 when it appears this serves as a reminder to
shift my consciousness, to pay attention and to be more present. At the
same time in reminds me of the sheer fallibility of conceptualization.
To understand something is to define it in your own terms, rather
than experience this same thing in its own terms. When I can abide
in this naked awareness I can then experience the world in the most
authentic, joyful and freeing manner possible.

I am obsessed with Hillary.

I am also obsessed with how much I hate Yoshinoya Beef Bowl.

As I walked out, they both jumped on me, and we had a threesome that night. Now I am obsessed with threesomes. They are so much fun! Go threesomes!

I am obsessed with serendipity, the color orange and the number 9.

Obsessed with Bones: "The Skull in the Sculpture":
It is GORGEOUS and I am OBSESSED with it!

I am obsessed with prehistory. Especially veloceraptors. I am obsessed with prehistory.

I am OBSESSED with jumpsuits and rompers, I can see why you would be hoarding them :)

Ohh, I am obsessed with figs! Figs! Figs!

I am obsessed with creativity and mosaics. I am obsessed with duck too!

YUM! onigiri! As usual, I am obsessed with cuteness and peace and what-not, but recently this pas week, I've come to be obsessed with ONIGIRI! it all started while I was reading Fruits Basket (duh!!! everything starts with Fruits Basket!) and the word ONIGIRI poped up every single page!! of course, knowing the superior knowledge of Fruits Basket, I though to myself "onigiri must be something really cool!" Well, as it turns out, onigiri IS something really cool!! It can be kawaii, cute AND nummy all at the same time! this was very exciting for me, so I went on an online search for onigiri and how to buy it. well, turns out you have to be in San Fran, NYC or Asia to get these cause they don't last very long…but you can make them!! I don't know why I like onigiri so much, and yet, I haven't even eaten one—I can't find any sea weed at super target. LOL—but you have to admit this is and AMAZING invention!! rice is so good, asian food is so good, sandwiches are so good, school lunches are SO BAD!!! so just take an onigiri with you!!! YUMMY! :)

My friends think I am obsessed with the topic of stuttering. I probably am. I go to continuous conferences on stuttering and have many friends and colleagues who stutter.

I am obsessed with pizza and believe that all pizza is good, but not all pizza should be called pizza.

I am obsessed with large squids. The boobs chapter was my favorite to write because (a) I am obsessed with my own and b) will talk about them at any juncture.

I Am Obsessed with Your Obsession. Lately I've been obsessed, and I'm starting to get obsessed about it. Not just my own obsessions but other peoples'.

I am obsessed with pure data. That's right. I love using pure data. It's my favorite hobby. I work on it more than anything, including schoolwork.

⮑ *DISMAY*

You didn't want me
to sidle up to the high
chthonic voltage, number
than frost, number than
the coiled attachments:
a kind of siphon
for this hamhanded
burgeoning. If I imitate
your enthusiastic rejecting
anxious beloved, can I
enter your hall of
repressed dismay? I can't
get her haircut: I don't
have that kind of hair.
I'm better than she is,
who does not think of you,
just as you do not think
of me. The world spins
on these bitternesses: my XXXX
for you offends me yet.

⤚ *SPLENDOR*

Maybe in the sandstorm of metaphor
you really don't have a body—
but there's something palpable
that makes me want to do battle
with your ectoplasmic splendor.
No alembic. Your body folds under you
as a collapsed puppet: my fervent
conquest of your gangliness now just
icky taxidermy. There are wings
under my armpits and also
secret beings. They straddle your
imagination in my imagination.
That is how we do not come
to know one another.

⮑ *Frozen Doe*

I guess I am improved by my peccadilloes,
their rabid squirming as fossils of affection
in the dumb sponge of heaving fixity. Every molecule
remembers a time before time, and if I open up
to receive all emotional messages (for example,
in my food), it's because that's the kind of maladroit
I am: preponed, animated, reticular, birdish. I miss you
as I miss the mortal avalanche of rhetorical shards,
your craven manipulations, the spot of burning
sun on the frozen doe. Everything catches fire
in the mangled frames of your irritability. You
don't love me? I don't know what you mean.
The hay is sweet—like me! — in these unfurled
taxonomies of pungent (but sensual) ridicule. You
don't love me? I don't know what you mean.
The murky planets sparkle in my ignorant hairdo.

agalma

the jewel inside the idol

➣ *Today's Ensemble*

Purpurated habitually: this delicate lunge.

Mellowly dramatic sparrows on my fluffed-up heartbeat.

The forge.

Reality went all glib and masturbatory ... like difficult money.

The poetry should TEAR UP the space (as a kind of scrounge). Right?

Ampling into a rough and beautiful future, not ignoring plumes.

Let me hold you as a hypnotized tongue.

Torrent of vibrant nos in the decorative blame arcade.

I couldn't sleep at all last night: like a fabric swan.

And on that weirdness now I lay my weary curls.

≥ *I Won't Be Adulthoodedness Anymore*

All I want is your little bouquet in the night,
Mr. "Art is art-as-art."

Is strobe's collective surprise still only for me?

Let reasonably "real" external manifestations of inner
nervous receptivity-of-impulse welcome me,

and yield with musically wired meat consciousness
the same fleeting "tawdriness" of other.

I am truly chiaroscuro glottal mucus slippage.

When I crush into the yang of trial dessert,
nonchalantly and impudently naked

Love begins to narrate its mechanical trickery in me

But there's only cellular messages at the apex
of American consumer fetishism.

Really, I can't exhaust language without you, my shaped tone!

I remember on your storm of dark jittery sparks to me

The day when you became my slowly uncoiling projector

Flickering me over with your haphazard composure.

I won't be pizzicato (MUTED form of plucking) or variable oval (actually unnameable) beautiful ruffled crisp language "sparrows,"— free from dogma and staged subservient "outsideness"—or a burst of white scratches … in anybody's brain-dance—anymore.

➤ *The Story About* **Cartoon Sight** *and* **Floozy Winds**

Is morning just a drastic plaything? Are the lords that blink on my
amniotic fallacy just hysterical cantors? Am I a cheerful donkey or hapless
surrogate? My hair needs to get swollen now with the foggy contrition of
seductive leeches.

Margarine paints the day a deathly boring upset green like the sounds
of the air in between bones where I huddle, an unsoothed monstrosity
in the conspiracy of soreness.

The thralls stick on me like the bubble paste of wildly aggressive submission.

Whenever the "graininess" hugs me in his styles-of-doubt, "glowing"
and "quivering" as flocks of white seagulls by the Gowanus Canal,

Gathering all un-idealized creations in one hush of dream at its dramatic
fiercest and most desperate quotidian,

It unites to the source of bounce-light—yawn-jaw's cartilage—rule-
encrusted eggs—a trance of motor-dictation to the "clown thumpers" …

And here I am, standing between "cartoon sight" and "floozy winds," a
visually discordant surface-fret in the uninentional law of poetry's
insane floppiness,

Trying to find an emptiness of nasal wind's hiss and moan, un-nouned,
a dark jittery bird, in your cold personality …

While the tremolo of morning sun sculpture, rhythmically castanet-like, sets
up a conflict that causes a tension that demands release from the spasmic
magma of hellish proprioception (oh and plus my money is sad like a horny
flower).

One aberration, a limp lettuce nightmare, is left inside the trembling
of the vocal chords' mottled bubbly shapes' pure negation, the forfeiture of
some vague code, like an animal fist in the plumpness of my radical fantasy:

that "felt-need-for," uh, spatially charged doodling — nerves
strumming-in-ear or tone-texture haunt:

numb thought's otherwise endless flights of fancy: "raw jewels" or
toned puddles...

crippled by error and its fixed, candy-colored pleasures: I believe in
the beauty of the singing, its thick, churning motion, its brave lipstick:
the lipid flash dance of your — how do you say? — *unbearable* ...
"outsideness."

➣ *I Need My Frolicking Angst Like a Sweet Elbow*

When curiously perverse sands fly by the farcical unrest as forms of egregious ellipsis, when my fears (iris-out) unleash traditional male genres unidentified oyster-shell voiceovers,

No words come out from my oblique dexterity or all-black music that merges with the sound of helicopters and the soft animals that are flatterers…

Seems it's only the gamine and quizzical shock cut, Oh Thou, God of dissolves and wipes.

Describe to me your favorite lounging clothes, bound as I am in (you know) "reading things into" these jarring effects.

To son of man I am but a basking calypso shark: Why Thou art destroy my expositional charm strategies and turbulent but fruity machismo?

Remember of one beautiful garden fill with rain as a commonplace, although fancy, phenomenon,

And how the holy frustrations of the underworld's adequately numerical flowers, adding value to the ritual sacrifice of its earthly puppet nature (the wing is the corporeal element),

Are only really nauseating for Thee,

A diabolically swashbuckling love one, confusing the moveable parts of relationships with the often shadowy extravaganza (like tons of cute lingerie) of spatial eternity in the beam factory, for already I am getting into dithyrambics …

Its tantalizing ruptures of brutal Divinity, its lowly human-powered contrivances.

My sense of smell is very delicate still in the corridors of uncertainty inside the germ of the wing.

Yet who can (who wants to) change my inflamed slice of life, my gleam and swirl, my vicious (but inverted) shuddering melody?

➷ My Inaudible Globular and Disjunctly Fretted Entanglement-of-Curves

Push me like a plethora of inexplicable visitations
Infer me deeply
Search my nervous extremity
Have I now be your flute-throat mate,
My sparkled optics' most immediate radiance?

I try to write you down my barest perspectival logic into the bottom of
cathectic thought till there's no more geo-classical ordering

This love letter (self's pulp of audible being) shall remind me

Meat ineffable love just as this far and it should be frank enough also.

Well, I wish the hypnogogically inspired of your organic blobs
to see you intrinsically variable always in the pulp of animal being

➤ *Now I Am Only Want to Say "Pharmokinetics."*
or
➤ *Give Me Your Liver*

Sometimes we make a deep cervical muscle, before it's too limp, don't hesitate to say to your love, "analgesia," but don't try to make the same muscle again.

Give me one chimp.
My ❧❦⚕❧ ,
Had you heard the nausea sing
The light of the analgesia touch our hand
A pain field of the living.

My ❧❦⚕❧:
Our first profound statement
is always military
A industrial love story

My ❧❦⚕❧:
Give me one neurophilosophy
Despite the low rates of somnolence
I am wincing
Expect you to come home as a folk construct

I wish I can fly into the toxicity
Together we may hear pluralogues
Now I am only want to say "pharmokinetics."

⮞ *In My Lustrelessness*

In my Lustrelessness, norm, form, and function are revealed as blithely editable, then turned into an intonation beyond the irrigated "pirate" mind.

I was sat with a malevolent question … but now I am more or less riotous and bounded, because, uh, the encounter between spectator-subject and image-object is a process of frivolous interference or mutual indignant mutation! I hope this doesn't sound too confrontational.

Don't know why the passive butterflies still hide in my messy entanglements, filled with the myriads who lived but never existed in the perverse bricolage?

Will everything become a blur in the afternoon? Can we tell a tiger from a mottled patch of shade in this lambent cacophony?

What a waste to chase the sun in this implausible account of mental life, like homemade fake puke … just as some white people envision breasts as (ontic) white, and go on to associate the latter with white screens.

If love poems are written in pidgin python in my dreams, there is also some polemic in some places, because all imagery is a bad riposte against the predictable triumph of "whimsy."

I will unite with the easterly wind's bum schemas and rattle-trap heuristics in the cocky dismissal of my lustrelessness, its impulsive body, the white nose of its prattling excess.

➤ *I am So Gory (Greeny) Today*

My emotions in a tremble, an enzyme in my tail
Whenever this love had been closed in a book of deceptive flashes,
Separated by three seconds of darkness in an invertebrate melodrama,
Just as rainbow that comes in a bad time for the females crawling
    down the grass,
Even though it pleases the male displays of antlers and feathers for the
    eye to see,
Truly, I am so gory (greeny) today, glowing like an adult,
Where am I gonna save my day from the gifts that form coils in a
    male's abdomen?

If my gullible legs aren't support me,
And my pulsing hands always say no or yes to nuptial gifts,
my life can go through the extra fog of cheap light and coiled forms,
like sticky traps equipped with lights that mimic courtship duets

(although if making light is so cheap for males, it seems odd that they
have not all evolved to be more attractive to females)
(I think the reason is ideological),

And round up in a dream the slowly starving blue female's
Flickering orange rain of bad-tasting chemicals.

⇒ *Song of the Radish-Eaters*

Here: a bouquet of buzzing diamond snakes.

The maenad slinks in, swinging her panther fur:
chakric inflammation.

Don't let the dog out. The dog is oily, and intimate,
and thirsty. Her gendered … minaret.

No fig jam for you, young lady.
You've been a very bad albatross.

A distant pig emerges from the
black space inside the brain, mouth open
in a little chuckle.

This lachrymal dried rose, its brittle
curses, flavor of grey air on my naked wrist.
My tongue's in the house of no. That's OK.

Light of life, pixies, fire, dancing elves, life, pixies, fire.

I've been a very selfish bacon. There's no bacon. I'm a
moon. I'm a moon, I'm a cow, I'm bacon. Conquering loss,
again and again … in the nude.

After the fire comes out, pull it into a shape of clay,
so it is like a ram's horn—or like a man.

Oh shit, too many grapes in my bra again,
no one cares.

Hamsters
roll around as maenads. Life is
twitchy. I'm twitchy. Needing
a glowy lingam to throw
milk at. Imminence quacks.

The train fills with Jews.

The environment does *bukkake* on me:
I have a neural spatter of dayglo prurience.

Love becomes a hollow vortex
in which a crippled monkey looks up briefly
with a mournful eye. We're all that monkey,
opening pupils to extreme blindness.

Loose locks: streaks
of objective correlatives
on a winter sky.

Lorn. Blue movies fill the fever factory,
chimneys spew white steam. I want a sleek
pink rooster or something salty here next to me,
vibrating essentialistly.

Can't … a symphony of … pheromones
… rouse … a long dry … salamander
from his … categories?

This is the song of the radish-eaters.

⇒ *Interclavicular*

Well. So that's how it is.
I take a long … hard … swallow.
When we talk, the whole world's
hollow, like a slimy rubber doll
delivered from my baser nature's
slumber. Rent asunder. Split:
me. Clone me. Anyway you want
me: small balloons of heaving breasts
pull me up to canny sky.
I have no license to fly
about the text with no
direction: it's a pail
of orgone butter that I flail in
with arms of lead. It's all
in my head. Put my head
back in your prance, my
orgone churn back in your silver
and illuminated discomfort. I like
my wounds: the woods are full
of tunes and subtle mavens.
The woods are also full
of ravens. They masturbate
the clockwork and the clockwork
sings for them. Peril. Mercy.
Mayhem—we're as alive
as any jaguar, those jaguars
with their powers of persuasion.
Let's talk about your dumb
evasion. It's like … that Ventures
song, that tumbly abrasion

of the string, the tick of hours
when we don't talk. Then
I show my cock like an irrational
coward spitting at a mirror. Love:
it agitates with fear. That's its
cruel demonstration, radical
and lush. And plush. It drives
insistent down the column
of a poem, writhing and strident.
It prods me with its trident,
pricks me with its allergenic
fluff. Have you had enough
of life, its ruddy seething
tension? One more thing I think
I need to mention: a smooth film
as a covering over parts that move
against each other? … or do I mean…
the art or practice of oblique sailing?
or just … a substance in the blood
of fireflies …? (hydrangeic, deuced,
russet, etc.?)

ᗌ *Form Dissolve*

Across from me on the train this morning
a woman reading "Folly"—not mine—something
written by a man with white hair, and in hardback.
Hard. Hardness. A synthetic creation turns into a living
creature thanks to color, and lighting, and visual effects,
whispering *come here, come here,* and *go away.* Peculiarity.
Pink filling, clear finish powder filling,
silk tips with powder, paraffin, buff, gel.
O these happy grey delusions: wisteria drooping
down on the stupidity of the besotted. Tearing:
the big fluffy dumpling of dissatisfaction.
I move into the flow of tears (big deal) like
another art experiment in the etiology of
decoration. Girls scrumptious as rice ...
the devilled day cares what I think ...
this is a Manhattan-bound trainwreck.
The city is spread out in its usual
panorama, the epidermis of capital
in plain sight. You are closed and open in your
usual way and the hop of love is stamping
meanly (as usual). "I want string cheese."
"I love string cheese." "Do I get to be the monster?"
I'm not too soulful for ... little destructions ...
the curative friend is art precisely BECAUSE
we are monkeys. The art is complicated
precisely BECAUSE we have woken up, and
we have woken up
                              because we will go to *sleep*
and that was my point at the beginning.
I don't care about cocks (so much) or bruises,

or that I'm all tangled. I'm not even sure
how much I care about you. (What did
you say your name was?) I care about
the TRANSOM—the air between us —
that little opening and the milky draft that got
through somehow. Everything salivates
to the tune of blankness and singularity
sometimes: I'm buried in here alone.
That's incurable: a woman is *of* love,
the bargirl is a frog, some people are
just born happy and others feel every
scrape and filing in the demon's lexicon.
Art as love. Pain. No more pain. Colored
lanterns: the experience of "wolving."
The spine curves on a feather. I wish
I were as beautiful as your cruel speech.
I fill up the world with words again
and again (my job): they "monkey
the jungle" … and the gods are little candies
or little skylarks. O this jealous devotion
to waxwork sense, the lie of sonic
embodiment, the list of "universes"
in the flailing mooncalf. There's something
cleaner than that, beyond your pat
"asymmetry" and cowboy rhetoric,
in the clumsy wash of being. Somewhere
a monk is rolling in iridescence and legroom.
Sex is like popcorn there and popcorn like
total overnight protection for the heavy flow
of ideation. It is indescribably boring that you
are not in love with me in the vermillion sea
of ebullient thinking. I like pain, really. Blue light
shines on the stupid trouble: the heaven faces

earthward as a lovely pessimism, and it doesn't matter
I'm a petulant freak like an orchid. It doesn't matter
because pain doesn't matter, it's a speckle on the death,
it's artificial like a nylon egg. The most free live love
doesn't scare anyone, it's like seaweed waving in fire.
Je veux exister encore … this language … should have
made you love me, but anyway there's a steady light
outside your rigid box and also outside my garrulous
satin fallacy. Your name will always be a shiver to me.
Now I need to sleep for a thousand years with a thousand
beautiful men —none of them you. The stars form a ring
around a beautiful device. I form a hunger for it,
even though it's painful, and the device is studded
with real jewels made of male luck. The luck
is strafing over my open mouth. "Is it nice out? It's
supposed to be nice out." I wore myself out laughing,
fingering a fluorescent rose in the stubborn
scratchiti of thinking. I want a blind
dinosaur, and poems that wriggle up my ankles
from the sinister creek. Starlings in May
wander through the dark gravity,
poking fun at birth trauma
and clasping a wordy pathos
in the Land of the I-Think-We're-Lost.

⮞ *O, the Magnet Sway of Knowledge*

O, the magnet sway of knowledge, fugitive
as laughing pard, vacuumed out of puny sighs
as the long moron argues ... aggravated legs,
perineum ... mad ploys ... I screwed, not up
not around ... the angry joy into the face of surface
aether ... with average banding ... this written "from
the heart" as lopsided tract ... the movement is holding ...
like fleas on a liminal stare, binge thinking ... always uncut
in pastel honorifics or glide stupor. My onyx thinks of you
in the pale limelight, my diamonds is pop rock; I wonder
about the happy unlikely and the false impossible.
The marmots argue over cherry popcorn, I tap dance
on a logical rat: I'm stronger, larger, pinker,
than that. The surplus smiles at the preeners,
and stinky sculptures spring up where there were none
before, and that's kinda cool in the prosodic tin(n)iness
of this cranial weltzschmerz, you know, I love
my dog I don't have a dog, I love the paper clock
that threatens sudden endings, I love the conversations
that play air guitar in my mordant memories. Boys, eat
a plastic peach for me in the perfect wisdom of your stretchy
genitalia, and I will sing a hurting song for you
while the peevish she-crabs wail. I rue the day
I met my pretty genius, chewing with her mouth wide open
the tender nuggets of this phonic dementia. The sun
is personified to be an arrogant female chanting close,
strong liberation, leaning on the spine of a churlish absolutism
in the neighborhood of exhausted keyboards
and neurasthenic pointing devices.

⤳ *Typical Poem*

He (not you) typed: "I'm in a relationship …
with everything." It sounds so sweet,
but all human beings are in bondage:
to each other. Thinking (then)
makes me squirt on a parallel bee:
this lachrymal honey. Poems may be
the pimples of the mind—I am
the fuschia frosting of the voice (I think),
and this is a cue to you to start paying
attention (to me) immediately! I retain water
as a swollen obduracy. The perfection
of wire fences and their pinkish insides.
Darling, when first we met, the lime
contention was an indignant sun. There is
pleasure all in and around me, knotted
through with infinity like a do-rag,
and I'm not hungry, or tired,
or lacking in entertainments, because
doing this entertains me. Even your
absence is amusing, a piquant musk
rubbed on the cusp of everything. I swear
undying love to the stripe on the street,
the dirty subway pole, the greek to-go cup,
the advertising insert, and of course
to homo erectus, *aww yeah*, his eager
condescension …

Something blurry in my imaginings today:
naked stork pictures, naked…
pictures, like I'm firing at my own sonar

echo in the dark. The naked metaphorical
clarity of gum wrappers … folded into tiny
dumb animals … so the rhapsodies now
turn inward, like condoms on ghosts.
Well, I had a yen for something in the dusky
confabulations of my anguished
iconicity, but that was pesky,
like all the inventive humans.
I love the beading on the edge of their
kameezes. You just bathe in the bitter
light. I notice that. I just notice that.
Everyone is "lumped in." You have
preferences, although not for me. I
like tea. I am a syrupy pariah with
such. beautiful. ears, and I pull all this
together! Yeah, rhapsodic cows always
hold babies in the cool midnight
against a million telephones that
vibrate against a billion babies: this body
just SEETHES with signification as a kind
of bugle … whither we are tending …
peach angel sleeves, and today I heart
the heat/ smearing neroli and civet
on meat.

A screw loose in the universal machinery:
like I care. Interpersonal machinery:
all the mean valentines! And you know
naked vultures have their own mean
valentines (I'm not soothed by this)
(or anything in the natural world).
Well, you have metallic emotions in
the listless absence. You battle

in buttery light, bite back as a
stone idol with a candy inside him
whereas I am a parasite who understands
"bell-like" perfection (bronze? plastic?),
and that's OK, in the way that everyone
on this train actually has a crotch.
It's (what's?) a vapid campanula—with
an eye. I burble the already-learned
coyness. "Art is my life," the identical
twins whisper to each other, stroking
(like foals) the pretty topiaries. Again.
And again.

⇒ *How High?*

Who knows that every bird that cuts
the aery way isn't some kind of
malevolent eaglet crashing through
the limbic system as a haughty dandy?
Hi there sweetie, *want some candy?*
Maybe I was wrong about everything:
the inner tubes, the clicking indicators,
the vital signs of the manipulators.
Suck.   My.   Lump. The fever sways
about like rhubarb: poison, but makes
a tempting pie … that frigid glint,
your bushy eye, its sharpened charm,
its arrogant impending harm.
The pixies knock about in the refrigerator,
wreaking havoc on the future toast.
I thought you were the most …
confusing … reptile … dictator … uptight …
aggravating … *ugh*: we play a game of
Twister™ there in the autonomous world of art
where all the selfish eaglets sing. "It didn't mean
a thing," I say to my refraction
in the mirror, and with a jeer I take up
fury's whiter icicle, but you take off
on your bicycle, breezy and slick.
You know, you're a prick, bothering me
till I'm all frothy like a pearl ham syrup
bellhop in the plummy midnight of this trans-
mutation. I fell for you in that stupid way
I fell for all the other stupid fuckers,
and here my pupils dilate into non-being.

Fighting and fighting, fleeing and fleeing.
Nemo stares at me with weird cat eyes.
Maybe he could take the eaglet by surprise,
and stand on his chest, perhaps, with this
ultimatum: love her, or leave her ALONE.
The sick clogged psyches of the lovelorn
thrash about on the special electric glass
sand of a special desert isle that is also
an offshore torture prison. So what if it is all
misprision? It's still … my experience,
bleak and wispy idols biting down through
epidermis into layers of steamy flesh,
which you have too though you won't admit
it, there in the freezing velvet of your slinky
mind. Here are some blood oranges
for your new kitchen. Please eat them with
this doggerel and a hornetswax candle
in the shape of a small woman with lots of
hair who is also fighting to be an autonomous
subject. The problem is, she's fighting in a sandpit,
just her, and all the little vipers, who are also
able snipers. Her skin, they say, *seems to think*.
She covers it in ink as charm protection: you
with your unctuous telephone voice and oh no,
no you don't the receivers are humming and
moist and I can't bear this endless strumming …
so … hmmm, I think I'll make a movie. I make
a movie of the grace of pain, of blind animals
and patchwork girls crawling along the raw
and clumsy surface of the mortal world, chums
of the unnameable. That yawning vibratory space.
Your face. Your face. Your face. You with your
creepy eaglet antics and horrible semantics:

I was "provocative" but not "alluring";
we had a "connection" but not a "bond" ...
I wave about as maidenhair frond ...
Because I can't sanely be near you I want
the potluck garbage of the mind to swell into a
crescendo of metallic roses that crash down around you
as a ritual burial and make these aerial sorties stop
already. Stop. Already. Stop. Stop. Stop.

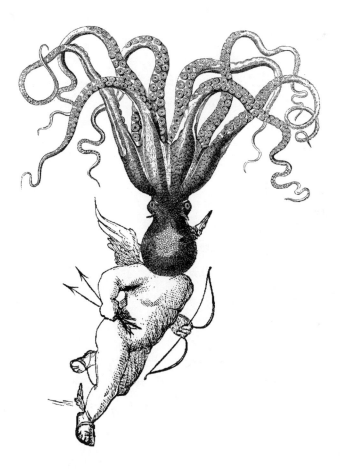

 **Blastopore**
(3/08/10)

Anyone came into this world
with a squirt of sticky coding and pain —
there's no avoiding that, comrade,
and I just have to tell you that, O elephant
I'm not thinking about in this psychic
room of convoluted tubules …
Primitive groove.
Trying and trying to put on
the big incognito sunglasses in the harsh light
of the cogito (neural crest) …
so there's that distance I bend over
into in the false early spring …
contorted, but not masochistically,
and not with contrition … I don't feel
contrite, but anyone's feeling is …
irritating. Chorion. Cleavage.
A radial cleavage that is indeterminate.
A membrane bulges outward. You know what you
need? A little … bird … because … who
cares … you were born. Cord blood. The lines cross
into opposite directions into different
abandoned lots (intervillios space) with junk
and new grass and ducts and cloacae and oh
I'm straining for some proper code
or beneficent felicitation in the face
of hostile you who developed and were born.
But I can't it, and that enrages me, your rage
(a knob-like thickening) enrages me,
so I weave this ugly potholder as occupational
distraction. Inner cell mass. Primitive knot.

Hey, the film is flapping, it's making that
flapping sound and it's time to change
the reel. I can't. Seem to. Change. The reel.
Did you know that cornification is a form of cell death
exclusive to the eyes? And Phenoptosis affects
many species, from yeast to salmon?
Look, the G train floor is covered with pastel
starfish, but ONLY I CAN SEE THEM (my sweet
misfortune). They are laughing at me! Hey!
They are laughing at me! Laughing.
Heart development. Development of the urinary
and reproductive organs. Cubical or prismatic
cells. The word EMPTY scratched on the side
of the seat then X'd out with black marker:
an observation, not an objective correlative.
Everyone is (duh) a dark mushroom.
Blonde in green, everyone has earbuds —
and was once a tiny zygote with DARK IRISES
alone in a liquid place. Then there's this forcing,
all these women SCREAMING and SWEATING:
they HEAVE and PUSH. Lines of hair on melon bellies.
Porous nipples. Eww. New nerve sensations. Life:
eww. Yolk sacs. Limb buds. First dryness and breath.
Smooth infants flail tiny limbs. Splanchnopleure.
Baby, each neonate is a locus of wild needs.
If I say I miss you I will feel sick so I won't
say it but time elapses and hapless we (duh)
are folded into it: irises, elephants, earbuds,
nipples, starfish, Wharton's jelly, everything.

⮑ *Sorry Universe*

(after Alli Warren)

I'm sorry for the way things are in China …

—John Denver

I kind of feel sorry
for the future of everything:
it isn't easy to shrug
with no shoulders. In the
universe we all feel like
outsiders, all computers
have had sex changes and
the vibrations of sub-atomic
particles are stretched out
sweaty spandex (the fabric of
space-time), by which I mean
it's just something I made
up as a joke. I'm so sorry
I'm just really upset
I can't find out what
the universe is … the
leopard universe's infinite
morbidity of the future
of everything. An alien bug
may or may not be benevolent
and the shape of the universe
is my horrible secret. That's why
I'm such a stud, considering
relative perspective to reduce
the margin of possible error.
Wow … more sex drama. Ooo.

It Means the World. I kind of
feel sorry for the future
of everything. I'm sorry,
but I'm really going to have to
kill you now.
I hope you don't mind.

⮑ *Convolvulus*

Confused. Should this book occasion
congratulations, or condolences?
Continuous consternation. But here it is:
a conglobed contrivance, a wild construct,
a papery concretion confounding reason
at every turn. I was "a very selfish bacon,"
it is true but also victim, in a sense,
of some fertile confluence or contretemps.
"Darling, when first we met, the lime contention
 was an indignant sun." A mere conversation
it seemed, at first, tinged with confession,
that quickly, for me, congealed into a "sensuous
confusion," contingent on "a black harmony of
conglomerates" that hid itself in every corner:
just as I turned around, it would be there,
a salt crystal "sun condor" preening its wing
in my peripheral vision, day and night,
a "convoluted tubule" of time. Imagination's
contours grew tangible: I felt them up. I went,
a pale conquistadora, "in fervent conquest
of your gangliness." You, "my dear contagion,"
with your "eager condescension," were controlled,
contemptuous, contractile, contrary, so of necessity
"the rhapsodies turned inward, like condoms on
ghosts," in my "musically wired meat consciousness."
Accordionly, I felt every "scrape and filing in
the demon's lexicon." It was all-consuming.
I couldn't sleep or concentrate, or eat much
more than consommé. Time disappeared in beloved
contemplation. All language contorted into a map

of connotations, a kind of conga line of unsoothed
monstrosities. I was never content. I couldn't consider
conscience or right conduct: something stronger
was controlling me. Something more (or less) than
conscious. Reader, so you know, there was no
consummation. Just limerence, infatuation, a crush —
but more than mere concupiscence: it was profound,
and sent me reeling, into *sound*: the incontinent heart,
here, in continent art — this wordy, contumacious
confectionary. Just me, consumed in phoenix flames and then,
reborn, concocting this: a kind of contact improvisation
against your contact inhibition. I convert the bitter ash
to cadence, conflict into careening conveyances,
and conundrums into singing nectar. I "conquer loss, again
and again, in the nude." "Is this just too confrontational? "
Too "gaudy, ostentatious, conspicuous, impudent?" Perhaps
it *was* all just concocted, confabulation, a mere conceit:
the icon 's jewel I thought I saw (a puddytat) inside of you.
(O,"fleeting tawdriness of other"!) Or maybe,
I was conned. Some things, though, escape
conceptualization, like "worm[s] without
a burning conclusion." And so, *confrere*,
I send this out upon its way,

con anima,

con brio,

con amore.

⇒ *Let This Heart Be Your Zoopraxiscope*

Darling

When I look into your abdication
There's an arbitrariness.
Let this heart be your zoopraxiscope
And move around your name

Darling
I've been deliquescing ….
Just a mumble of lines
You'll unscrew me

I can't undo my cerebellum
Can't retire my lyric
Seems so freaky
To take you out of me

sorry you couldn't get drunker

pouring honey down a well

ROOF BOOKS
the best in language since 1976

- Arakawa, Gins, Madeline. **Making Dying Illegal**. 224p. $22.95.
- Dworkin, Craig, editor. **The Consequence of Innovation: 21st Century Poetics**. 304p. $29.95.
- Eisenhower, Cathy. **would with and**. 120p. $13.95
- Retallack, Joan. **Procedural Elegies / Western Civ Cont /**. 120p. $14.95
- Fodaski, Elizabeth. **Document**. 80p. $13.95
- Guest, Barbara. **Dürer in the Window, Reflexions on Art**. Book design by Richard Tuttle. Four color throughout. 80p. $24.95.
- Mohammad, K. Silem. **The Front**. 104p. $13.95
- Reilly, Evelyn. **Styrofoam**. 72p. $12.95.
- Shaw, Lytle, editor. **Nineteen Lines: A Drawing Center Writing Anthology**. 336p. $24.95

ROOF BOOKS are published by
Segue Foundation
300 Bowery • New York, NY 10012
For a complete list of titles visit our website at
seguefoundation.com

ROOF BOOKS are distributed by
SMALL PRESS DISTRIBUTION
1341 Seventh Street • Berkeley, CA. 94710-1403.
Phone orders: 800-869-7553
spdbooks.org